Expect
The
Best

No-Nonsense Wisdom That Works!

Chuck Coté

Published by Pathfinder Press
3805 Wrenwood Ct.
Midland, MI 48640

Publisher's Cataloguing-in-Publication Data
Coté, Chuck.

Expect the best : no-nonsense wisdom that works / Chuck Coté. –
Midland, MI : Pathfinder Press, 2004.

p. ; cm.
ISBN: 0-9754775-0-1

1. Self-actualization (Psychology) 2. Attitude (Psychology)–Quotations.
3. Happiness–Quotations. 4. Excellence–Quotations.
5. Quality of life–Quotations. 6. Motivation (Psychology)–Quotations.
7. Success–Quotations. I. Title.

BF637.S4 C68 2004   2004105929
158.1/02--dc22   CIP

Cover and interior design by CQG! Chrystique Graphics, chrysq@ejourney.com

Printed in the United States of America
08 07 06 05 04 • 5 4 3 2 1

Dedication

This book is dedicated to my son Charles.

*You have a fantastic sense of humor,
a passion for living life to the fullest,
and the perseverance to stay the course
no matter how rough the journey.*

I'm intensely proud of you because you do …
Expect The Best!

I love you!
Dad

Acknowledgments

Over the years many people encouraged me to write this book. I can't begin to name all of them but I want to take this opportunity to thank a few.

First, I want to thank Diane Papendick at Pendell Printing who collected and typed thousands of quotes that we used for "The Thought For The Day."

Thanks also to JoAnn Baumann at Pendell who, in addition to being an excellent executive assistant, gave me dozens of inspiring quotes and ideas.

Vic Osteen of Win Seminars Inc. deserves my gratitude because, as a superb agent, he challenged me to make *Expect The Best* an outstanding book.

I give my most heartfelt love and appreciation to my beautiful wife, Josie. No matter what obstacles, setbacks or problems we face, you are always an incredible source of strength and support for me. I thank God for blessing me with you because the two of us are enjoying an amazing life!

Introduction

At Pendell Printing Inc. in the early 1990's we implemented the Total Quality Management System from Dr. W. Edwards Deming. I was responsible for gaining our employee's commitment for the change and from that mission came "The Thought For The Day."

To help expand our employee's expectations I looked for inspirational and motivational ideas to support our initiative. Every day I posted them as "The Thought For The Day" on a plaque outside my office.

Initially a few people were curious about the daily messages but before long a steady stream of employees were coming by my office to read them. Many of them told me that the messages made them think about what was possible for them personally as well as professionally. We had so many requests for copies of the quotes and ideas, that we began publishing them in our company newsletter.

Since then countless people have encouraged me to write a book using these messages. I finally took their advice and *Expect The Best* is the result.

My intention in writing *Expect The Best* is to provide ideas and suggestions, quotes and questions, that stimulate your thinking, raise your expectations and challenge you to discover new ways to enjoy life.

This no-nonsense wisdom works for me and I hope it works for you too.

Expect The Best!

Chuck Cote'

and now...

Expect
The
Best

1.

Do your best
doing what you love to do.
You'll be immensely successful
and incredibly happy.

2.

"Men are born to succeed not fail."
- Henry David Thoreau

3.

You have to go through the obstacles
to get the opportunities.

4.

"To err is human, but when the eraser
wears out ahead of the pencil,
you're overdoing it."
- Josh Jenkins

5.

"Everybody wants to know what I'm on. What am I on?
I'm on my bike, six hours a day busting my butt."
- Lance Armstrong

6.

Commitment separates winners from losers.

7.

We wouldn't worry so much about
what other people thought of us,
if we knew how seldom they actually did.

8.

"Don't aim for perfection.
Strive for excellence!"
- Chuck Coté

9.
The mind is
like a parachute;
it functions best
when it's open.

10.
It's okay to fall down
just make sure you get up.

11.
*"The way I see it, if you want the rainbow,
you gotta put up with the rain."*
- Dolly Parton

12.
Be proud of yourself for who you are,
not for what you do.

13.
Don't ask someone to do something
you wouldn't do yourself.

14.
Always deliver more than you promise.

15.
*"Only those who risk going too far
can possibly find out how far one can go."
- T. S. Eliot*

16.
Mental exercise and flexibility are the keys
to developing a strong mind.

17.
*"I have never been disabled in my dreams."
- Christopher Reeve*

18.
Praise people publicly.
Coach them privately.

19.
Don't litter in other people's lives.

20.

"Expect The Best
and
take responsibility
for
getting it!"

- Chuck Coté

21.
If someone says "don't worry,"
you better.

22.
*"Adolescence is that period in kids' lives when their
parents become more difficult."*
- Ryan O'Neal

23.
When talking with a teenager,
remember that you were one once.

24.
*"Even if you're on the right track,
you'll get run over
if you just sit there."*
- Will Rogers

25.
"Happiness is a habit; cultivate it."
- Norman Cousins

26.
People don't care how much you know,
until they know how much you care.

27.
"A hunch is creativity
trying to tell you something."
- Frank Capra

28.
Learn to trust your instinct and intuition.

29.
Don't wait for things to happen.
Make them happen!

30.

People who are responsible and accountable get results.

31.

"To find success;
go where others won't go,
do what others won't do,
and be what others won't be."
- Chuck Coté

32.

Make a list of the things you want to do before you die
and start doing them.

33.

"A journey of a thousand miles
begins with a single step."
- Lao-Tzu

34.
Choose your spouse carefully.
It is a life changing decision.

35.
*"One can never consent to creep
when one feels an impulse to soar."*
- Helen Keller

36.
Quality people do quality work.

37.
*"Life is like riding a bicycle.
You don't fall off unless you stop pedaling."*
- Claude Pepper

38.
Get in shape!

39.

*"Doubt whomever you will
but never doubt yourself."*
- Christian Bovee

40.

Stay away from negative people.

41.

*"Many of life's failures are people
who did not realize how close they were
to success when they gave up."
- Thomas Edison*

42.

Make sure you have at least one
good friend you can talk to.

43.

At least once in your life
work as a waiter or waitress.

44.

Never get into a business deal with someone
you don't like or trust.

45.

*"Do what you can,
with what you have,
where you are."
- Theodore Roosevelt*

46.

Say "please" and "thank you" a lot.

47.

Life is too short to carry a grudge.
You only hurt yourself,
not the person you're mad at.

48.

Drink in moderation or don't drink at all.

49.

Make it a habit to be on time.

50.

*"We must believe the things
we teach our children."
- Woodrow Wilson*

51.

Every day tell your children,
"I love you."

52.

Keep a $100 bill in your wallet
for emergencies.

53.

*"Without discipline, there's no life at all."
- Katherine Hepburn*

54.

Learn to balance your checkbook
and keep it balanced.

55.
*"Don't complain.
Don't explain.
Just get it done!"*
- Chuck Coté

56.

When you get up every day,
thank God you're alive.

57.

Remember people's names.

58.

*"Seek first to understand
then to be understood."*
- Stephen Covey

59.

Spend 20% of your time on a problem
and 80% on the solution.

60.

"Scared money don't make no money."
- Greg Sheaffer

61.

Go to church, any church, on a regular basis.

62.

If you're lost, stop and ask for directions.
It beats driving around aimlessly.

63.

*"People have one thing in common;
they are all different."*
- Robert Zend

64.

Clean out your drawers and closets
once a year.

65.

Every day tell your spouse,
"I love you."

66.
"Beauty is not caused. It is."
- Emily Dickinson

67.
Put photos of your family and friends
on your refrigerator.

68.
At least once in your life
do some type of a sales job.

69.
"All I can say about life is,
Oh God, enjoy it!"
- Bob Newhart

70.
Get a physical exam every year.

71.
Don't be busy; be effective.
You'll live longer, make more money
and have more fun.

72.
"Nobody ever died of laughter."
- Max Beerbohm

73.
Give something back to your community.
Do volunteer work.

74.
"God has given us two hands,
one to receive with
and the other to give with."
- Billy Graham

75.
*"You can achieve excellence
or make excuses,
but you can't do both."*
- *Chuck Coté*

76.
If something is worth doing,
it is worth doing well.

77.
Be sincere when you give a compliment.

78.
Say "thank you" when you
get a compliment.

79.
*"Abundance is being rich,
with or without money."*
- Suze Orman

80.
When you don't agree with the government,
write your congressman or senator.

81.
If you do it right the first time,
you won't have to do it over again.

82.
"Be a yardstick of quality.
Some people aren't used to an environment
where excellence is expected."
- Steven Jobs

83.
Don't expect people to think like you;
they're human beings too.

84.
"Do not take life too seriously.
You will never get out of it alive."
- Elbert Hubbard

85.

When you buy a book put your name
and the date on the inside front cover.

86.

Give books as gifts
and write a note to go with them.

87.

*"There are two ways of spreading light;
to be a candle or the mirror that reflects it."
- Edith Wharton*

88.

Watch less TV.

89.

Rome wasn't built in a day
and neither will you.

90.

Never talk about someone behind their back
and beware of people who do.

91.

Always take the high road
no matter what someone else does.

92.

*"Live so that you wouldn't be ashamed
to sell the family parrot to the town gossip."*
- Will Rogers

93.

Learn how to make one food dish
that is your specialty.

94.

Go skinny dipping at least once in your life.

95.

"There is a difference between disappointment and doubt, and it's a big difference."
- *Chuck Coté*

96.

"Make yourself an honest person.
Then you can be sure
there is one less rascal in the world."
- Thomas Carlyle

97.

Don't lie, cheat or steal.
You may think no one knows,
but someone does.

98.

Don't blame anyone or anything
for your problems.
Take personal responsibility for them.

99.

"Life is like a ten-speed bike.
Most of us have gears we never use."
- Charles Schulz

100.
There ain't no fair!
Get over it.

101.
*"My father taught me that the most powerful
weapon you have is your mind."*
- Andrew Young

102.
Wear clothes and shoes that make you
look and feel your best

103.
Smile more than you frown.

104.
Laugh more than you cry.

105.
"The unexamined life is not worth living."
- Plato

106.
When you're open to receive,
it's amazing what comes your way.

107.
*"If you obey all the rules
you miss all the fun."*
- Katherine Hepburn

108.
Once in a while enjoy a day
doing wild and crazy things.

109.
Do what you say you will do!

110.
Success is good;
significance is much better.

111.
Always remember:
"dust you are and to dust you shall return."

112.
*"Don't go around saying
the world owes you a living;
the world was here first."*
- Mark Twain

113.
*"If you want to kill an idea,
get a committee working on it."*
- Charles Kettering

114.
"The best thing about being alive
is you get to do stuff."
- Chuck Coté

115.
What can you do today
to make your life amazing?

116.
Go to Washington DC at least once
in your life to see our nation's capitol.

117.
Driving too fast or too long
is too dangerous.

118.
Don't sweat the small stuff.

119.
"Reading is to the mind,
what exercise is to the body."
- Joseph Addison

120.
Read good books.

121.
If you want to achieve excellence,
think differently.

122.
Make a plan for your life and work it.

123.
"As you build confidence
you destroy barriers."
- Chuck Coté

124.

*"Always bear in mind
that your resolution
to success is more important
than any other thing."*
- Abraham Lincoln

125.
Use your God given talents and abilities
to serve others.

126.
Every day learn
something new from someone new.

127.
You can learn a lot
from the young and the old.

128.
"Try? Do or do not. There is no try."
- Yoda from "Star Wars"

129.
Treat people with dignity and respect.

130.
"Success is simply a matter of luck.
Just ask any failure."
- Earl Wilson

131.
Don't dwell on your mistakes.
Learn from them and move on.

132.
Be careful when using the word "but."
It negates everything you said before it.

133.
Don't drink and drive
and don't ride with someone who does.

134.
Be happy and enthusiastic.

135.
When you're in love, be in love;
don't be half-hearted about it.

136.
Be kind and considerate.

137.
Read "The Power of Positive Thinking"
by Dr. Norman Vincent Peale.

138.
Vote!
It's our most precious right.

139.
"Drink good wine but buy it on sale."
- Ann-Charlotte Fleischer

140.

*"I am convinced that life is
10% what happens to me and
90% how I react to it."*
- Charles Swindoll

141.

Don't try to please everyone,
it's impossible.

142.

Don't be boring. Be original.

143.

*"Keep your eyes and your ears open,
and your mouth shut,
and you'll make it as a Marine,
because you've got what it takes."*
- My Marine Recruiter

144.

*"One man can make
a difference and
every man should try."*

- John F. Kennedy

145.

If you've done everything you can,
then "let go and let God."

146.

A positive anything is better
than a negative nothing.

147.

"Life is a question
and it's up to us to live the answer."
- Chuck Coté

148.

Send handwritten notes.

149.

Every day tell your parents,
"I love you."

150.
*"Feeling sorry for myself
is a luxury I cannot afford."*
- Stephen King

151.
Don't have "pity parties."

152.
*"Husbands are like fires;
they go out when they're left unattended."*
- Cher

153.
Passion ignites motivation.

154.
To succeed in life you need
focus, passion, dedication and perseverance.

155.
*"Fear is that little darkroom
where negatives are developed."
- Michael Pritchard*

156.
Don't get too wrapped up in success.

157.
Don't get too frustrated by failure.

158.
*"It's a funny thing about life;
if you refuse to accept anything but the best,
you very often get it."
- Somerset Maugham*

159.
Focus your attention on your intentions.

160.
*"If you want a particular quality or habit,
act as if you already have it."*
- William James

161.
Stand up for what you believe in.

162.
Tip well when you get good service.

163.
*"Be who you are and say what you feel,
'cause people who mind don't matter,
and people who matter don't mind."*
- Dr. Seuss

164.
Look at people when you talk to them.

165.
*"Common sense
is not so common."*
- Voltaire

166.
Don't jump to conclusions;
the fall back to reality hurts.

167.
Read something inspirational every day.

168.
*"Challenges make you discover things
about yourself that you never really knew."*
- Cicely Tyson

169.
Carry photos of your loved ones.

170.
*"If you don't enjoy your life,
who will?"*
- Chuck Coté

171.
Have a firm handshake.

172.
*"What you think of yourself is much more
important than what others think of you."*
- Seneca

173.
"No" is a complete sentence.

174.
*"Why not go out on a limb?
Isn't that where the fruit is."*
- Frank Scully

175.
When you think you can't go on,
go on anyway!

176.
"Celebrate success.
Survive setbacks.
Learn from both."
- Chuck Coté

177.
"When people talk, listen completely.
Most people never listen."
- Ernest Hemingway

178.
Become a great listener.

179.
"Never give in.
Never. Never. Never. Never."
- Winston Churchill

180.
Live with an *Expect The Best* mindset.

181.
Be a goal setter and a goal getter.

182.
*"It's good to have an end
to journey towards; but it is the journey
that matters, in the end."*
- Ursala K. LeGuin

183.
Walk and talk with confidence.

184.
*"You can't build a reputation
on what you're going to do."*
- Henry Ford

185.
Become a good storyteller;
it's a simple way to make a point.

186.

*"Opportunity is missed
by most people because
it is dressed in overalls
and looks like work."*
- Thomas Edison

187.

Don't win arguments; build relationships.

188.

"It may be those who do most,
that dream most."
- Stephen Leacock

189.

Always use good table manners.

190.

Don't play the "blame game."

191.

"Be just as enthusiastic about the success of
others as you are about your own."
- The Optimist Creed

192.

*"Never play cards
with a man called Doc.
Never eat at a place
called Mom's.
Never sleep with a woman
whose troubles are
worse than yours."*
- Nelsen Algren

193.

When using a cell phone
be courteous and considerate.

194.

*"Try not to become a person of success
but rather a person of value."*
- Albert Einstein

195.

Make time to pray and meditate.

196.

*"I always wanted to be someone,
but I should have been more specific."*
- Lily Tomlin

197.

Everyone smiles in the same language.

198.

If you think you don't make a difference, think again.

199.
"Our life is what our thoughts make of it."
- Marcus Aurelius

200.

Nothing is opened more often by mistake,
than the mouth.

201.
"Happiness is a matter of your own doing.
You can be happy or you can be unhappy,
it depends on how you look at things."
- Walt Disney

202.
Make positive self-talk
your daily conversation.

203.
*"Always do sober what you said
you'd do when drunk. That will teach you
to keep your mouth shut."
- Ernest Hemingway*

204.
Vulnerability is a wonderful quality to have.

205.
Age is mostly a matter of mind.
If you don't mind, it doesn't matter.

206.
Perform random acts of kindness.

207.
"Act as if it were impossible to fail."
- Dorothea Brande

208.
Be a person who is
responsible and accountable.

209.
No one on their deathbed ever wished they
had spent more time at the office.

210.
*"Surround yourself only with people
who are going to lift you higher."*
- Oprah Winfrey

211.
Go forward with faith, not fear.

212.

*"In life, some people
believe they can,
some people
believe they can't,
and they're both right."*
- Henry Ford

213.

*"It's not the strongest of the species
that survive, nor the most intelligent,
but the most responsive to change."*
- Charles Darwin

214.

A wise man learns from his own experience;
a wiser one from the experience of others.

215.

There are no shortcuts to success.

216.

"What we prepare for is what we shall get."
- William Graham Sumner

217.

Always wear your seat belt.

218.
"The only reason I took up jogging was so that I could hear heavy breathing again."
- Erma Bombeck

219.
Find an exercise program you like
and stick to it.

220.
Don't smoke! It could save your life.

221.
"Failure is never final unless you quit.
Never quit!"
- Chuck Coté

222.
Some people are just a pain in the neck.

223.
Take lots of family pictures
and put them in albums.

224.
*"True success is overcoming the fear
of being unsuccessful."*
- Paul Sweeney

225.
Smart leaders hire smarter people.

226.
*"No matter how much cats fight,
there always seem to be plenty of kittens."*
- Abraham Lincoln

227.
*"A word to the wise
ain't necessary.
It's the stupid ones
who need advice."
- Bill Cosby*

228.
Don't blame your mother!

229.
"Only those who dare to fail miserably
can achieve greatly."
- Robert F. Kennedy

230.
If you ask someone to help you,
they usually will.

231.
Make sure you have a good accountant.

232.
Celebrate your birthday.

233.
*"Challenges are
the questions.
Results are the answers."*
- Chuck Coté

234.
*"When you are not afraid to die,
then you are really ready to live."
- Chuck Coté*

235.
Use your time and money wisely.

236.
Many a fool passes for a wise man
by keeping his mouth shut.

237.
*"It is better to live rich,
than to die rich."
- Samuel Johnson*

238.
Every so often just relax.

239.

*"It doesn't take a hero
to order men into battle.
It takes a hero to be one of those men
who goes into battle."*
- Norman Schwarzkopf

240.

Honor the men and women
of our armed forces.
They protect our freedom.

241.

*"When you get to the end of your rope,
tie a knot and hang on."*
- Franklin D. Roosevelt

242.

There is a difference between sarcasm
and a sense of humor.

243.
*"The quality of a person's life is in
direct proportion to their commitment to excellence,
regardless of their chosen field."*
- Vince Lombardi

244.
Thank a police officer.
Thank a fireman.
Thank a nurse.

245.
Don't go east looking for a sunset.

246.
*"Freedom to do your best means nothing
unless you're willing to do your best."*
- Colin Powell

247.
It's more fun to laugh than to cry.

248.
"Invest in the human soul. Who knows,
it might be a diamond in the rough."
- Mary McLeod Bethune

249.
If someone made a difference in your life,
tell them how much you appreciate it.

250.
"If God is your co-pilot, switch seats."
- Billboard

251.
Learn how to dance,
then dance like no one is watching.

252.
Learn to say "No."

253.
*"Show me a person who has never
made a mistake, and I'll show you
someone who has never achieved much."*
- Joan Collins

254.
Thank a teacher.

255.
Be passionate and enthusiastic.

256.
*"You can't sweep other people off their feet,
if you can't be swept off your own."*
- Clarence Day

257.
Some days are more difficult than others.

258.
"Choices have consequences;
choose wisely."
- Chuck Coté

259.
Give time and money to worthy causes.

260.
"You can't pray a lie."
- Mark Twain

261.
Never forget September 11, 2001.

262.
Enjoy good food.
Enjoy good friends.
Enjoy good food with good friends!

263.
*"One of the blessings of old friends is that
you can afford to be stupid with them."*
- Ralph Waldo Emerson

264.
Never wrestle in the mud with a pig.
You're both going to get dirty,
but the pig likes it.

265.
Protect your reputation.
It is one of your most valuable assets.

266.
Most of us know what to do;
but we don't always do what we know.

267.
"Don't worry. Be happy."
- Bobby McFerrin

268.
Keep your car clean and running well.

269.
*"If you judge people
you have no time to love them."*
- Mother Theresa

270.
The only difference between
a rut and a grave are the dimensions.

271.
Hell hath no fury like a woman scorned.

272.
Love and lust are two different emotions;
make sure you know the difference.

273.
*"We must constantly build dykes of courage
to hold back the flood of fear."*
- Martin Luther King Jr.

274.
In life don't be too careful or too careless.

275.
When you play a game,
play to win but play fair.

276.
"Everyone who has taken a shower has had a good idea. It's the person who gets out, and does something about it who makes a difference."
- Mike Owens

277.
*"The reason worry kills more people
than work, is because more people
worry than work."*
- Robert Frost

278.
Use the internet wisely.

279.
*"What hunger is in relation to food,
zest is in relation to life."*
- Bertrand Russell

280.
Don't ignore health problems.

281.
Mean dogs have mean owners.

282.

"Results? I've gotten a lot of results.
I know several thousand things
that won't work."
- Thomas Edison

283.

Keep holiday traditions alive
by sharing them.

284.

Eat more fruits and vegetables
and less junk food.

285.

"Some succeed because
they are destined to.
Most succeed because
they are determined to."
- Anatole France

286.
When you work; work.
When you play; play.
Don't confuse the two.

287.
"It is better to wear out than to rust out."
- Richard Cumberland

288.
Life is as much fun as you make it.

289.
Enjoy a sunny spring afternoon.

290.
A clean desk is the sign of a sick mind;
but it is more efficient.

291.

Remember that you are a work in progress.

292.

*"You were born an original.
Don't die a copy."*
- John Mason

293.

Share everything, including chocolate.

294.

*"Choose to be the love-finder
rather than the faultfinder."*
- Gerald Jampolsky

295.

One of the sweetest sounds anyone hears
is their own name.

296.
No whining!

297.
"If you want to make God laugh,
tell Him your plans."
- The Talmud

298.
What you sow is what you reap,
good or bad.

299.
"It is better to be looked over,
than to be overlooked."
- Mae West

300.
Leaders lead people. Tyrants push them.

301.
Don't run red lights or stop signs.

302.
Eat healthy foods in moderation.

303.
"People often say motivation doesn't last.
Neither does bathing,
that's why we recommend it daily."
- Zig Ziglar

304.
Don't be afraid to express your faith in God.

305.
"God does not ask your ability or inability.
He only asks your availability."
- Mary Kay Ashe

306.
"If you don't like something, change it.
If you can't change it, change your attitude."
- Maya Angelou

307.
"Snowflakes are one of nature's most fragile things; but just look at what they can do when they stick together."
- Ronald Reagan

308.
Read to your children.
You are giving them a priceless gift.

309.
Great leaders *Expect The Best*
from themselves
and the people around them.

310.
"If angry, count to ten before you speak.
If very angry, count to one hundred."
- Thomas Jefferson

311.
If someone asks you a simple question,
give them a simple answer.

312.
*"If you can't get out of it,
get into it."*
- Outward Bound Motto

313.
When you make a commitment,
live up to it.

314.
*"You never know what is enough,
unless you know what is more than enough."*
- William Blake

315.
"In any job you are expected to do,
do more than is expected of you."
- Chuck Coté

316.
Yesterday is gone and you ruin
tomorrow by worrying about it today.

317.
Avoid lawsuits.
They are expensive and nobody wins.

318.
"Do not let what you cannot do
interfere with what you can do."
- John Wooden

319.

*"If you can give
your son or daughter
only one gift,
let it be enthusiasm."*

- Bruce Barton

320.
A difference of opinion
is exactly that and nothing more.

321.
*"God grant me the serenity
to accept the things I cannot change,
the courage to change the things I can,
and the wisdom to know the difference."
- The Serenity Prayer*

322.
Don't ignore problems.
Deal with them quickly and effectively.

323.
If all you have is your health,
you have all you need.

324.

*"My scalpel is only so sharp,
and I'm only so good.
What's ultimately going to be
the deciding factor
in our beating this disease
is your positive attitude,
your outlook,
and your determination."*
- Gregory T. Wolf, M.D.

325.
Never give up hope.
Miracles happen every day.

326.
"I hear and I forget.
I see and I remember.
I do and I understand."
- Confucius

327.
Drive safely and defensively.

328.
Enjoy a good vacation every year.

329.
"Productive Meetings" is an oxymoron.

330.
Continuously learn and improve;
it's a wise investment in yourself.

331.
*"He who can't be counseled,
can't be helped."*
- Benjamin Franklin

332.
Have the courage to ask for advice
when you need it.

333.
"Nothing is so much to be feared as fear."
- Henry David Thoreau

334.
Lighten up and live longer.

335.
*"I listen to critics because often they are
a good source of information for
what you have to do differently."*
- John Chambers

336.
We think and act not according to the truth
but the truth as we perceive it.

337.
What would your life be like,
if you didn't worry so much?

338.
*"A leader has the vision and conviction
that a dream can be achieved. He inspires the
power and energy to get it done."*
- Ralph Lauren

339.
"You can't please all people;
some people just don't want to be pleased."
- Jack Johnson

340.
Spend less than you make
or make more than you spend.
Either one will work.

341.
Never say "or I'll die trying"
unless you mean it.

342.
"You may be disappointed if you fail,
but you are doomed if you don't try."
- Beverly Sills

343.
Enjoy a variety of recreational activities.

344.
*"He that cannot forgive others, breaks
the bridge over which he must pass himself;
for every man has the need to be forgiven."*
- Thomas Fuller

345.
Send a funny card to someone.

346.
*"The ability to express an idea is as
important as the idea itself."*
- Bernard Baruch

347.
Learn how to give a speech or presentation.

348.
"You can be both a dreamer and a doer by removing one word from your vocabulary; 'impossible'."
- Robert Schuller

349.
When you greet someone,
smile and look them in the eye,
extend your hand and say "hello."

350.
Don't go to places that allow smoking.
Secondhand smoke is a silent killer.

351.
*"The easiest thing in the world to be is you.
The most difficult thing to be
is what other people want you to be."*
- Leo Buscaglia

352.
*"No matter how old a mother is,
she watches her middle-aged children
for signs of improvement."
- Florida Scott-Maxwell*

353.
Don't argue with your mother-in-law;
you won't win.

354.
Be unique … because you are!

355.
When you borrow something, return it.

356.
In life, pain is a given;
suffering is a choice.

357.
*"You should never
have more children
than you have car windows."*
- Erma Bombeck

358.

Be humble but don't put yourself down.

359.

Be a good winner and a gracious loser.

360.

"No matter how limited your vocabulary,
it's big enough to let you say something
you'll later regret."
- Adlai Stevenson

361.

No matter who you are
or how old you are,
you don't know everything.

362.

Love your friends and know your enemies.

363.
*"Two roads diverged
in the woods and I,
I took the one
less traveled by
and that has made
all the difference."*
- Robert Frost

364.

"The motto should not be:
forgive one another;
rather, understand one another."
- Emma Goldman

365.

Other people rarely change
until we change how we treat them.

366.

Give flowers to someone
for no reason at all.

367.

"Destiny is not a matter of chance;
it is a matter of choice.
It's not something to be waited for;
it is something to be achieved."
- William Jennings Bryan

368.
Be careful when someone says,
"the check is in the mail."

369.
*"It's not the size of the dog in the fight,
it's the size of the fight in the dog."
- Dwight D. Eisenhower*

370.
Don't put a cute message
on your answering machine.

371.
When you watch a July 4th celebration
think about what it represents.

372.
Enjoy your life and the people around you.

373.
Success leaves clues. Look for them.

374.
*"If you are going to tell people the truth,
be funny or they will kill you."*
- Billy Wilder

375.
Be friendly to everyone you meet
because your paths may cross again.

376.
*"We know nothing about motivation.
All we can do is write books about it."*
- Peter Drucker

377.
Cash is king. Credit cards are killers.

378.
"Empty barrels make the most noise."
- Sister Celine Marie

379.
When you say "don't take this personally"
to someone, you can bet they will.

380.
"Behold the turtle. He makes progress
only when he sticks his neck out."
- James B. Conant

381.
Laugh for no reason at all.

382.
"In times of stress, be bold and valiant."
- Homer

383.
When in doubt, pray.
If still in doubt, pray harder.

384.
Nothing is more annoying
than when someone continues talking
while you're interrupting them.

385.
*"There's no way to be a perfect mother and
a million ways to be a good one."*
- Jill Churchill

386.
Don't let the "arrogance of success"
or the "curse of perfection" trap you.
Instead, go forward with
the "wisdom of excellence."

387.
*"Imagination is
more important
than knowledge."*
- Albert Einstein

388.
"To play it safe is to not play."
- Robert Altman

389.
Hold yourself to a higher standard
than anyone expects of you.

390.
*"You can't expect to hit the jackpot if you
don't put a few nickels in the machine."*
- Flip Wilson

391.
Be your spouse's best friend, lover,
soulmate, playmate, and confidant.

392.
Don't be too proud to say, I made a mistake.

393.
"Go big or go home!
No one is promised tomorrow.
Live for today!"
- Branden Wyman

394.

You're only here for a short time,
enjoy the journey.

395.

Only you can make your life truly amazing.

396.
"I don't know the key to success,
but the key to failure
is to try to please everyone."
- Bill Cosby

397.

*"Excellence is to do
a common thing
in an uncommon way."*
- Booker T. Washington

398.
*"I'd rather have thirty minutes of wonderful
than a lifetime of nothing special."*
- From the movie "Steel Magnolias"

399.
*"The surest way to love anything is
to realize it might be lost."*
- G. K. Chesterton

400.
Respect other people's opinions
even if you don't agree with them.

401.
*"Choose a job you love and you will never
have to work a day in your life."*
- Confucius

402.

Ignorance is not bliss, it's just plain stupid!

403.

"A fool and his money are soon parted."
- Proverbs

404.

A wise man is not too proud
to ask for advice when he needs it.

405.

Read the fine print before signing anything.

406.

"It is not enough to have a good mind;
the main thing is to use it well."
- René Descartes

407.

What we put out in the world
is what we get back.
What are you putting out?

408.

*"Ask and it will be given to you;
seek and you will find;
knock and the door will be opened."*
- Luke11:9

409.

Ask yourself better questions
and you get better answers.

410.

*"Rudeness is a weak person's
attempt at strength."*
- J. Matthew Casey

411.
Throw your heart into a project
and your mind and body will follow.

412.
Write a book to share
your thoughts and ideas.

413.
*"A real friend is one who walks in
when the rest of the world walks out."*
- Walter Winchell

414.
Laugh a lot.
Cry a little.
Don't take yourself too seriously.

415.
"Saints are sinners who just kept on going."
- Robert Louis Stevenson

416.
Your work is a personal portrait of yourself.

417.
If something doesn't come up
the way you want,
you have to forge ahead."
- Clint Eastwood

418.
Life is too short to sit on the sidelines.
Get in the game!

419.
Recycle. It's good for the earth.

420.

*"Class is an aura of confidence
that is being sure without being cocky."
- Ann Landers*

421.

Keep a success journal of key victories in
your life and review it often.

422.

Develop good credit and keep it that way.

423.

Don't rain on someone's parade.

424.

If you think education is expensive,
try ignorance.

425.
*"Everything is funny as long as
it is happening to someone else."*
- Will Rogers

426.
As long as you can laugh at yourself,
you'll always have an audience.

427.
*"We cannot become what we need to be
by staying what we are."*
- Max Depree

428.
Give a copy of this book to someone.

429.
Leave well enough alone,
unless you really want to deal with it.

430.
Listen to educational tapes and CD's.

431.
*"When one door closes, another one opens;
but often we look so long and so regretfully
upon the closed door, that we do not see
the ones which open to us."*
- Alexander Graham Bell

432.
If something sounds too good to be true,
it probably is.

433.
"Here is the test to find whether your mission on earth is finished: if you're alive, it isn't."
- Richard Bach

434.
The only job where you start at the top, is digging a hole.

435.
"If you're gonna be a failure, at least be one at something you enjoy."
- Sylvester Stallone

436.
Write a will and update it periodically.

437.
*"The time is always right
to do what is right."*
- Martin Luther King Jr.

438.

"You can change behavior in an entire organization, if you treat training as a process rather than an event."
- Edward Jones

439.

Keep a pen and paper
by the side of your bed so when
you wake up during the night with an idea,
you can write it down and go back to sleep.

440.

"Courage is doing what you're afraid to do.
There can be no courage
unless you're scared."
- Eddie Rickenbacker

441.

Listen to good music.

442.
"Luck is a matter of preparation
meeting opportunity."
- Oprah Winfrey

443.
If you are stressed out, ask yourself;
"What is the cosmic significance of this?"

444.
"Always put the cherry on top."
- Richard Pendell Sr.

445.
Some minds are like concrete;
all mixed up and permanently set.

446.
Don't tell someone they look sick or tired.

447.
*"It is never too late
to be what you might have been."*
- George Eliot

448.
Find a good insurance agent and buy enough
insurance to take care of your family.

449.
*"Don't look back;
something may be gaining on you."*
- Satchel Paige

450.
*"Our doubts and fears
are our worst enemy."*
- William Wrigley Jr.

451.

Instead of being your own worst enemy,
start becoming your own best friend.

452.

Go the extra mile, it pays off.

453.

*"Getting the truth in the New York Post
has been as difficult as finding
a good hamburger in Albania."*
- Paul Newman

454.

The news we see and hear
is the media's interpretation of the news.

455.

Get to know your neighbors.

456.
"If you have never been hated by your child,
you have never been a parent."
- Bette Davis

457.
Obstacles are those frightful things you see
when you take your eyes off your goals.

458.
"Most people would rather get affection
than give it."
- Aristotle

459.
Don't be afraid to hug people
and say you love them.

460.
Follow the K.I.S.S. rule.
Keep It Simple Stupid!

461.
*"The toughest thing about success is
that you have to keep on being a success.
Talent is only a starting point.
You have to keep working on that talent."*
- Irving Berlin

462.
"The first wealth is health."
- Ralph Waldo Emerson

463.
If you get a serious health diagnosis,
get a second opinion.
If the two differ, get a third one.

464.
*"You are only as good
as the people you hire."*
- Ray Kroc

465.
Take frequent walks to clear your head.

466.
Think with your mind; love with your heart.

467.
*"A bank is a place that will lend you money
if you can prove that you don't need it."*
- Bob Hope

468.
Make sure you have a good relationship
with your banker.

469.
*"When you
stop making excuses,
you start getting results."*
- Chuck Coté

470.
*"No one is useless in this world
who lightens the burden for someone else."*
- Charles Dickens

471.
Never give advice to someone
unless they ask for it.

472.
*"There is nothing we receive with so
much reluctance as advice."*
- Joseph Addison

473.
After all is said and done,
more is usually said than done.

474.

"Never confuse a single defeat
with a final defeat."
- F. Scott Fitzgerald

475.

Being alone is different than being lonely.

476.

"To love oneself is the beginning
of a lifelong romance."
- Oscar Wilde

477.

You better believe in yourself
or no one else will.

478.

Today is a gift; use it wisely.

479.
Get your priorities straight.
If you don't, who will?

480.
*"The trouble with the rat race is,
even if you win, you're still a rat."*
- Lily Tomlin

481.
Sometimes you have to say
enough is enough.

482.
*"There is only one success;
to be able to spend your life
in your own way."*
- Christopher Morley

483.

"Love doesn't make the world go around.
Love is what makes the ride worthwhile."
- Samuel Easton

484.

Whose ride do you make more worthwhile?

485.

"Love is not love until love's vulnerable."
- Theodore Roethke

486.

Love like no one is watching.

487.

"When the eagles are silent
the parrots begin to jabber."
- Winston Churchill

488.

"Never go to a doctor
whose office plants have died."
- Erma Bombeck

489.

Good doctors are dedicated
to helping their patients.
Find one.

490.

Don't see a doctor who won't take the time
to talk to you and answer your questions.

491.

"To be pleased with one's limits
is a wretched state."
- Johann Wolfgang von Goethe

492.
*"No one
can make you feel inferior
without your consent."*
- Eleanor Roosevelt

493.

Play with children and remember
what it was like to be a child.

494.

*"Pretty much all the honest truth telling
there is in the world
is done by children."*
- Oliver Wendell Holmes Sr.

495.

Good leaders encourage people.
Bad ones discourage them.

496.

*"Live as if you expected to live
a hundred years, but might die tomorrow."*
- Ann Lee

497.

When you leave this earth … leave a legacy.

498.

*"What would you attempt
if you knew you could not fail?"
- Robert Schuller*

499.

Watch a sunrise and a sunset over an ocean.

500.

*"When you realize you want to spend the
rest of your life with somebody,
you want the rest of your life to start
as soon as possible."
- Billy Crystal*

501.
Nothing in this world is perfect, including this book.

Parting Thoughts

In *Expect The Best* I hope you found some no-nonsense wisdom that works. I'm always looking for new material for future editions of *Expect The Best* so please send me your ideas and suggestions, quotes and questions.

Expect The Best!

To have Chuck Coté speak to your organization call:
(800) 350-7695

To order any of Chuck's books or products call:
(989) 837-3553

Or go to:
www.chuckcote.com

Chuck Coté

No-Nonsense Wisdom That Works

Chuck Coté challenges people to *Expect The Best And Get It!*

Chuck's business experience is in both the corporate world and as an entrepreneur where he has started four companies.

He is also a cancer survivor who knows how to overcome difficult challenges and enjoy life.

Chuck is a graduate of Michigan State University and before college spent three years in the Marine Corps and served a tour of duty in Vietnam.

He is a member of the National Speakers Association and the National Speakers Association of Michigan.